ENGLAND

THE PANORAMAS

ENGLAND

THE PANORAMAS

MARK DENTON

CONSTABLE · LONDON

To Samuel James Denton

Sorry, this is why you haven't seen too much of daddy for the last few years!

Constable & Robinson
3 The Lanchesters
162 Fulham Palace Road
London W6 9ER
www.constablerobinson.com

First published in the UK in 2010 by Constable, an imprint of Constable & Robinson Ltd

A copy of the British Library Cataloguing in Publication Data is available from the British Library.

ISBN 978-1-84529-969-9
1 3 5 7 9 10 8 6 4 2

Printed in Malaysia

CONTENTS

FORELAND POINT, LYNMOUTH

INTRODUCTION

How does one photograph England? It's a question that has preoccupied me for the past five years. I remember when I volunteered to shoot a book on the Lake District, I sat down afterwards and thought, 'There's rather a lot of it. This is going to be tough.' Ultimately you get through it, and for the most part it's extremely enjoyable. First, though, you need to make a start. As in climbing a Lakeland fell before first light, it's the first steps that are the toughest. The task is as much psychological as physical: as the legs and lungs are struggling to cope with the initial slope, the brain is not yet fully alert. Once one reaches the summit, however, it's almost plain sailing – just a case of watching one's feet.

Shortly after completing the Lake District book, I was discussing future projects with my editor. I'd previously suggested a huge project on the whole coastline of Britain. On this occasion his response was, 'How about just England?' Just the coast of England, I was thinking, that doesn't sound too bad. Soon, however, I realized that this was not to be a book on just the coastline of England; it was to include all the bits in between as well. I managed to disguise my inner disquiet, but afterwards I needed a sit down and a hot cup of tea.

The way to tackle such a project is to work backwards from the finished product. No book could possibly contain thousands of photographs; this one contains just over a hundred. Although I may, in the end, have taken a couple of thousand photographs, the project had to begin with these final hundred or so images in mind.

It is not difficult to find inspiration in England. Curiously, many English people seem a little blinkered when it comes to their own country. Many rarely travel beyond their home town or place of work other than to catch a plane to somewhere sunnier. I'm surprised that such travellers don't take a greater interest when they return, for it is then that it always strikes me what a remarkable island this is: extraordinarily green and fertile. The verdant colour is so vivid that the difference, compared even with close neighbours such as France, is palpable. Seen from a height of 35,000 feet, the Seven Sisters and Beachy Head appear as a tiny crust, a scratch of chalk on a blackboard, on the edge of vast acres of greenery.

So after my cup of tea, I began to draw up lists and plans for all the places I would visit, realizing that the project was actually a good fit with my normal modus operandi. A photographer friend of mine, rather more celebrated than myself, can ramble around his local area endlessly, shooting remarkably different and original versions of the same geographical features again and again. I'm much more of a collector. Almost invariably, once I've photographed a place and am happy with the result, I prefer to move on. For this book, I could simply work through the gazetteer of England, filling in all the places I wanted to visit, but as yet hadn't: the magnificent buildings, the soaring cliffs, the (occasionally) snow-capped peaks. The scale of the plan was daunting, but there was only one thing to do: start booking hotels, and – guiltily – putting miles on the car: the paradoxical, but unavoidable, cost to the environment of recording such beauty.

This is England – my misty-eyed rendition of it, at any rate. It is not 'real' – no collection of photographs could ever do justice to the entire country, and any negative aspects are absent. This, though, is how I choose to represent it.

WEST

I first visited the West Country as a child, making the long train journey from the North East with my grandmother to spend a week in Torquay on the English Riviera. I was to return on many subsequent occasions. Indeed, it's the only area of the country where I've actually lived, apart from the North East and Yorkshire, where I have moved around the same small corner of England what seems like a hundred times. When I moved to Bristol in 1997, while getting on with a nine-to-five job, I managed to visit, for the first time, places such as Clevedon, Bath, Lyme Regis and Stonehenge. Although work soon took me back to my comfort zone in the North East, I always felt I had unfinished business in exploring the West Country, even in those pre-camera days.

In 1999, the total eclipse provided the perfect excuse to make the long trip. After a car journey which seemed to last an eternity, we finally arrived at an unashamedly rustic farmhouse, tucked between the fields inland from Newquay. At that stage I was just beginning to discover my true vocation, though my limited and rather shoddy collection of 35 mm equipment was never likely to capture any worthwhile images. In terms of location, however, it seems I was already switched on; I insisted that we would view the eclipse from the cliffs at Bedruthan Steps. When the moment came the weather was bitterly disappointing: the cloud was so thick as to allow only tiny glimpses of the sun, and these were of a disc so dim that it could comfortably be viewed with the naked eye – the eclipse itself was entirely obscured. And yet, as an experience, I would never forget that day. Gradually the darkness

above us became complete, in the distance the street lights of Newquay flickered on, while close to the horizon a tiny ring of light shimmered in every direction. The feeling was remarkably claustrophobic, as if a gigantic black canopy had descended on us. Seabirds squawked and the collective gasp from the assembled viewers was audible. Photographically speaking, the sea stacks of Bedruthan had been unable to add anything to the experience; the tide was in preventing access to the beach, but it was certainly an unforgettable place to view such an event. Undoubtedly there will be no repeat of the experience on English soil in my lifetime, but I'm already pondering a trip to the Faroe Islands for 2015.

The occasion had provided me with a few gloomy photographs of the rock stacks from the cliff top, and a single image taken with a poor quality zoom lens of a partially eclipsed sun, filtered by thick cloud. Only now though, am I beginning to understand the impact the experience had on me and my future career. It confirmed my love for landscape, and also the importance of being in the right place at the right time. This is the key to everything I do today, and of far greater importance than any item of camera gear.

The following year I began shooting still life with a 35mm camera, and within two years my obsession with the English landscape was well underway. Buying my first panoramic camera, in 2003, was a race against time in order to be able to shoot an annular eclipse on the Yorkshire coast, although when I received the camera I quickly discovered that the 105mm lens was far too wide to record the sun in any detail. Nevertheless, that day in the west had been a pivotal day in my life, and I soon realized where my future career lay.

THE SECRET PATH, GOLITHA WOODS

CLASSIC VIEW OF STOURHEAD

TO SEA AT PERRANPORTH

DARK CLOUDS, CLIFTON SUSPENSION BRIDGE

FOOTPRINTS AT BEDRUTHAN STEPS

LATE SUNLIGHT ON HAMELDOWN, DARTMOOR

SUMMER CLOUD ABOVE BRENT TOR

SUBLIME DAWN, SALCOMBE

SUNRISE BEYOND CORFE CASTLE

ROCK LINES AT MUPE BAY

ROYAL CRESCENT IN AUTUMN, BATH

SCULPTED CLIFFS, BURTON BRADSTOCK

EVENING LIGHT, AVEBURY STONE CIRCLE

GOLD HILL, SHAFTESBURY

INTENSE SPRAY AT THE COBB, LYME REGIS

ST ANDREW'S, CORTON DENHAM

THE SCOVARN ROCK, MULLION COVE

BOATS AT MOUSEHOLE HARBOUR

THE TIN MINES OF BOTALLACK HEAD

CLEVEDON PIER AT SUNDOWN

DURDLE DOOR AND THE COAST PATH, ISLE OF PURBECK

HEART

The bones of perhaps the best known Englishman of all, William Shakespeare, lie in the Holy Trinity Church in Stratford, next to the River Avon, in what might fairly be regarded as England's heart. Geographically speaking, it's not far off, and perhaps England's cultural heart lies here, too.

I like the idea that it is a playwright, Shakespeare, who embodies England in a way that other Englishmen – from kings to lager louts – don't. It was in Stratford that I felt I was beginning to get to grips with England and the huge project I had undertaken. I knew, of course, that it would be impossible to 'define' the country in a single volume, but I had just started on the task in earnest and this seemed as good a place as any to start.

It had been a grim winter, not especially cold, but continually dark and grey. I was in Stratford for the wedding of friends and had taken my camera bag along more in hope than in expectation. Miraculously, on the one morning when I could shoot, the clouds parted for what seemed like the first time in two weeks, revealing a perfect frosty winter morning. Normally, I might have been a little prissy about the complete absence of cloud, but on this occasion I was more than ready to accept the gift of some sunshine. The shot was obvious: the sun was ideally positioned to warm the bare willow branches and the famous church on the far bank. The only question in my mind related to the length of exposure. Fortunately, the conditions afforded me the luxury of two options: either I could use a short exposure to freeze mirror-like reflections on the river, or I could use a longer exposure which would slightly blur the trees and the stonework. I opted for the latter. The scene was precise and manicured, a world away from the rugged landscapes of the north, but this too was England: a formal, correct beauty, largely man-made.

In much the same way as Shakespeare gave form to the raw material of human life, the English have crafted their own landscape, embellishing it with remarkable buildings and gardens. This extends beyond individual buildings to entire communities such as villages like Lower Slaughter and Bibury in the Cotswolds. At the other end of the architectural spectrum come the distinctive skyline of Liverpool and Blackpool's homage to the Eiffel Tower.

The heart of England does not lack for natural beauty. The high rolling hills of Shropshire and Herefordshire provide a superb archetype of the English countryside, while the northern areas are dominated by the rugged stone backbone of the Pennines. It is here, in the Ribble Valley at the foot of the mountain of Whernside in North Yorkshire, that a man-made structure enhances the landscape perhaps better than anywhere else in England. The twenty-four arches of the Ribblehead Viaduct on the railway between Settle and Carlisle, built between 1870 and 1874, surely stand as one of the greatest of all creations of the Victorian industrial age. It seems impossible to imagine that anything similar today would be carried out with such grandeur and panache, a reminder of how recently Britain dominated the world in technology and engineering. Those days may be gone, but their legacy lives on in this sublime structure.

AUTUMN EVENING, BOLTON ABBEY

HOLY TRINITY CHURCH, STRATFORD-UPON-AVON

IRONBRIDGE IN AUTUMN

ENTRANCE TO GORDALE SCAR

GOLDEN LIGHT ON CURBAR EDGE

SUNBURST OVER HAZELTON CLUMP

MORNING CLOUD, THE LONG MYND

RIBBLEHEAD VIADUCT FROM BATTY MOSS

AUTUMN DAWN AT SYMONDS YAT

HEREFORD CATHEDRAL AND THE RIVER WYE

THE RIVER WYE AT TINTERN

WINTER COLOURS, LOWER SLAUGHTER

LIGHT ON BRIMHAM ROCKS

SUNRISE, DYNELEY FARM

TWILIGHT HUES, BLACKPOOL

VIEW FROM CAT'S BACK RIDGE, HEREFORDSHIRE

WARWICK CASTLE AT DAWN

WHIRLPOOLS, BEEZLEY FALLS

NORTH

I don't think I would have become a photographer if I hadn't been raised close to the sea in the North of England. My childhood home was a five-minute downhill run or bike ride from the North Sea. It was normally too cold and windy to actually sit on the beach, but I became intrigued by the landscape almost as soon as I was allowed to leave the house by myself. I would ride up and down the coast and walk along the rocky beach as far as the village of Whitburn, careless of tide tables as I would not be now.

My psyche was shaped by the sea. I loved foggy evenings, when I would lie in bed and listen to the rhythmic foghorn of Souter Point Lighthouse, which sounded both scary and reassuring. My bedroom window looked out onto the local cemetery, giving rise to the familiar joke that we had 'quiet neighbours'. I would read ghost stories such as *The Watch House* by Robert Westall, set in the former coastguard station in nearby Tynemouth, feeding my imagination with mystery and intrigue. My first camera was an instamatic which used old, square-format 126 cassette film. Curiously, most of my first photographs were of buildings like the Watch House and Tynemouth Priory rather than of members of my family.

Getting to explore the region beyond my immediate area took a little longer. These days, I would think nothing of jumping in the car and driving to Cornwall, but when I was a child, going to Middleton-in-Teesdale for my first holiday felt like a major expedition. That owes much to the era, when cars were far more expensive in real terms; after my grandfather died – when I was just two – the family never owned one. So travel meant a lot of fuss, and suitcases, and being at bus or train stations at least half an hour too early.

I remember two school trips being particularly inspirational, given that most such trips seemed to be to amusement parks. One trip was to the Kielder Forest for a walk in the rain, followed by lunch in Berwick, then rolling in the sand dunes at Bamburgh and even a final stop-off at Seahouses, my first experience of the truly spectacular coast of Northumberland. I'm not sure how we squeezed all that into one day, but I'm equally sure that I didn't imagine it. The second, a year or two later, was to Ullswater, the second largest of the English lakes and widely regarded as the most beautiful. I remember being a little disappointed that we hadn't seen the 'heart' of the Lake District or its largest peaks, but perhaps that was simply an indication of how much I'd been interested by what we had seen. Our trip by steamer down the lake from Pooley Bridge and back again seemed to keep the rabble quiet, but I'm not sure the same could be said of the bus-ride home. I think it culminated in a sing-song to keep the troops out of mischief. It's quite remarkable how clear these memories are, given the amount of time that has passed. Although revisiting the places certainly refreshes the memory, and can often can reshape it, individual aspects of those days are still vivid.

Without being conscious of it at the time, these experiences were whetting my appetite for the English landscape. I wanted to see more of it. Perhaps growing up got in the way, however, because I was 21 before I returned to the Lake District. I had no real Alfred Wainwright-style 'revelatory' moment; I just found each Lakeland experience intensely memorable – the effect was incremental rather than instantaeous. I will always regard the whole of the North of England as my home turf rather than just the small corner in which I was raised.

DAWN ON THE DUNES, BAMBURGH

BLUE MILLENNIUM, RIVER TYNE

BLENCATHRA FROM LOW RIGG

DAWN BLUES, PLACE FELL AND ULLSWATER

BORDER HILLS AT YETHOLM

THE FELLS IN WINTER, FROM DALE HEAD

TRANQUILLITY, CRAG LOUGH

ALNWICK CASTLE AT DAWN

CLEARING RAIN OVER RYDAL WATER

FIRST LIGHT ON CATBELLS AND THE NEWLANDS VALLEY

SUNRISE OVER THE FARNE ISLANDS

INTO THE LIGHT, DUNSTANBURGH

CLASSIC VIEW OF DURHAM CATHEDRAL

ROSEBERRY TOPPING AT DUSK

MAY MORNING, TARN HOWS

SNOWS ON SKIDDAW, FROM SKELGILL BANK

ST MARY'S LIGHTHOUSE, WHITLEY BAY

SUMMER STORMS ABOVE HADRIAN'S WALL

LIGHTBURST OVER LADY'S RAKE, DERWENTWATER

SOLITARY TREE, HIGH CUP NICK

THE BLEAK LAKE, COW GREEN RESERVOIR

EAST

The east coast of England is under attack; each year some of it is lost. The coastline at Holderness, in East Yorkshire, retreats an average 1.5 metres a year, faster than just about anywhere else in the world.

At Hornsea, the extent of the problem is clear. Defended by a sturdy concrete promenade and groynes on the beach, the town is beginning to jut out from the surrounding coastline, which, undefended, has continued its retreat. Astonishingly, parish records show that coastal defences were attempted as early as the fourteenth century, nevertheless many buildings and whole towns have already been lost to the waves along this coast.

As well as being composed of a mixture of crumbling clay and soil deposited during the last ice age, the eastern coastline of England is exposed to relatively strong waves. Two million years ago, before the last ice age, none of the land currently disappearing existed; the coast ran in a series of chalk cliffs from Flamborough Head down the edge of the chalk wolds. The sea is only gradually reclaiming what it once lost.

Even inside the Humber Estuary, the aptly renamed 'Sunk Island' was dry land until relatively recently. My great-grandfather was stationed near here during the Second World War, at Kilnsea and Spurn Head, where he had an easier time of it than some, looking out for Germans who, in the end, never came. The huge concrete fortifications defending the mouth of the Humber Estuary against enemy attack, in which he once lived, are now being humbled by the natural force of the waves.

Only in a handful of places, such as the Yorkshire and Lincolnshire Wolds, the North York Moors and the Lincolnshire Ridge, on which Lincoln Cathedral stands, does the east of England rise much above sea level. The cathedrals of York and Ely tower up from these plains to rival that of Lincoln, and the skies, with little on the horizon to obscure them, appear to stretch forever. I'd been sceptical of claims that the light in East Anglia is extraordinary, but the east of England enjoys lower rainfall and more sunshine than much of the rest of the country and there is little pollution. As the sun approaches the horizon its light passes through more of the Earth's atmosphere, and here in the flatlands, there is simply less to get in the way of that filtered red and yellow light.

In Happisburgh a whole street is gradually crumbling into the sea, and its fifteenth-century church will eventually be lost. I stood in the disintegrating garden of an abandoned bungalow at the cliff edge and took a shot along this new coastline for posterity rather than artistic merit. By a cruel irony, owners are deemed responsible for demolishing their own doomed houses before they topple off the cliff, in case they should fall on someone below.

The east coast of England is a reminder of the transience of this land mass. Geographically, as well as culturally, England has not always existed. It has in the past sunk beneath the waves, risen again, been covered and uncovered by ice sheets, shifted on tectonic plates and split from its adjacent continental mainland. A significant rise in sea level could see England split into thousands of islets. If Norfolk and East Yorkshire do disappear beneath the waves one day, it seems certain that it will be only to return in some new and exciting form. Our own future, by comparison, feels even more precarious.

SHARP DAWN LIGHT, SELWICK'S BAY

SEPTEMBER SKIES, BURGHLEY HOUSE

FROSTED DAWN, LONDESBOROUGH PARK

SUNRISE AT SOUTHWOLD PIER

HOT AND COLD, FAIRYDALE

LIGHT AT BRANCASTER STAITHE

SUMMER CLOUD, KING'S COLLEGE, CAMBRIDGE

AUTUMN GLORY, BISHOP BURTON

SKY DRAMA, LINCOLN CATHEDRAL

SHIMMERING TIDES, HUNSTANTON

SUMMER LIGHT IN ELY

LATE SUMMER SKIES AT WHITBY HARBOUR

TWIN STORMS, HUNMANBY, EAST YORKSHIRE

WINTER MAJESTY, ROBIN HOOD'S BAY

SOUTH

For me the south of England was the undiscovered country, where most of the clichés of what is quintessentially English appear to be generated. I had taken a number of photographs in London for a previous book, but all I had really were preconceived ideas of how the south should look. I was determined, though, that this should not be a book of cityscapes, nor of stately homes. It is the natural landscape that most interests me, although that includes the most outstanding efforts to marry architecture to that landscape.

Naturally I headed for the iconic white cliffs, with the theme from *Dad's Army* and a thousand commercials for washing powder or car insurance repeating in my head. Given my love for coastlines, I knew they would be spectacular, but my first brief visit to Seaford was not a resounding success, with gloomy skies ruling out any display of light. No time looking at landscape is ever wasted however. Did I realize that the sublime curves of the Cuckmere River and the marvellously tranquil estuary were adjacent to England's most recognizable coastal feature?

My second visit was rather better. The sky broke up above the Belle Tout lighthouse, and distant shafts of light were visible from Seaford Head. When I sat later in the rickety, scaffolded café at Birling Gap, enjoying an unexpectedly good cup of coffee, it felt as if the day was somehow a defining moment of the whole project. The light was still gloomy, but the clouds were beginning to break apart and I could sense my luck beginning to change. I drove back to Beachy Head, where clouds were forming intriguing patterns beyond the headland. Reaching the top of the cliff I found flowers laid in memory of those who had taken their lives jumping from there. As light flickered through the cloud base and formed patches on the sea, I immediately shot the whole scene. A few months later I heard of a couple who had leapt to their deaths from Beachy Head, distraught at the death of their young son. Few news stories have ever affected me so greatly.

I'm not a great one for revisiting the same place again and again, but the Seven Sisters and the Cuckmere Estuary were different. On my third visit the tide was distant and I was shod in my wellies, as I should always be for coastal work. The skies were annoyingly clear; I had hoped for more cloud to fill the panoramic frame with dynamism. It did occur to me, though, faced with those cliffs kept white by daily erosion and rock falls, that perhaps a 'blank canvas' in the skies above might be preferable, focusing the eye on the main subject. I used reefs near the cliff of Seaford Head as a foreground, before venturing further and further out onto the shingle to look back at the wall of white stretching to the east. As the sun declined, I finally found the right spot, near the outer edge of the outflow of the Cuckmere River. Further north on the beach, the river can be too deep for wellies-wearing photographers, but in the spot I had chosen it spreads out, creating a mirror-like surface which reflects the cliffs. The Seven Sisters went from being a piercing, bluish white, to yellow, to pink, to violet, before reflecting the blue of twilight. I shot all of these moods, no doubt using far more film than I needed too, before finally trudging the mile or so back up to the Seaford Head car park.

The mission to photograph England was finally drawing to an end. The feeling on that pivotal day at Birling Gap, many months previously, had been that of reaching the summit of a climb and beginning the descent; this felt like catching sight of the welcoming hostelry at the end of a full day of walking. A few more minor hurdles remained to be overcome, but this was it. It was time to move on, taking only my photographs and memories with me.

CLOUD FORMS BEYOND BEACHY HEAD

AUTUMN COLOURS AT SCOTNEY CASTLE

MARY AND JOSEPH, CAMBER SANDS

THE CASCADE, VIRGINIA WATER

SOUND MIRRORS OF DENGE, DUNGENESS

MIST ON THE RIVER ARUN, ARUNDEL

MORNING SUNLIGHT, LANCING COLLEGE

RADCLIFFE CAMERA AND ST MARY'S CHURCH, OXFORD

CLOUD MOTIF FROM DEVIL'S DYKE, SOUTH DOWNS

DURHAM CLINCH THE TITLE, CANTERBURY

WILD PONIES OF THE NEW FOREST, LYNDHURST

DAWN FROST AT BODIAM CASTLE

MORNING SKIES, ROCHESTER CATHEDRAL

DAWN SHADOWS AT STONEHENGE

THE NEEDLES FROM ALUM BAY, ISLE OF WIGHT

SPRING GLORY AT DUNCTON HILL

THE WEST PIER AT BRIGHTON

STORM SHADOWS, BURY HILL

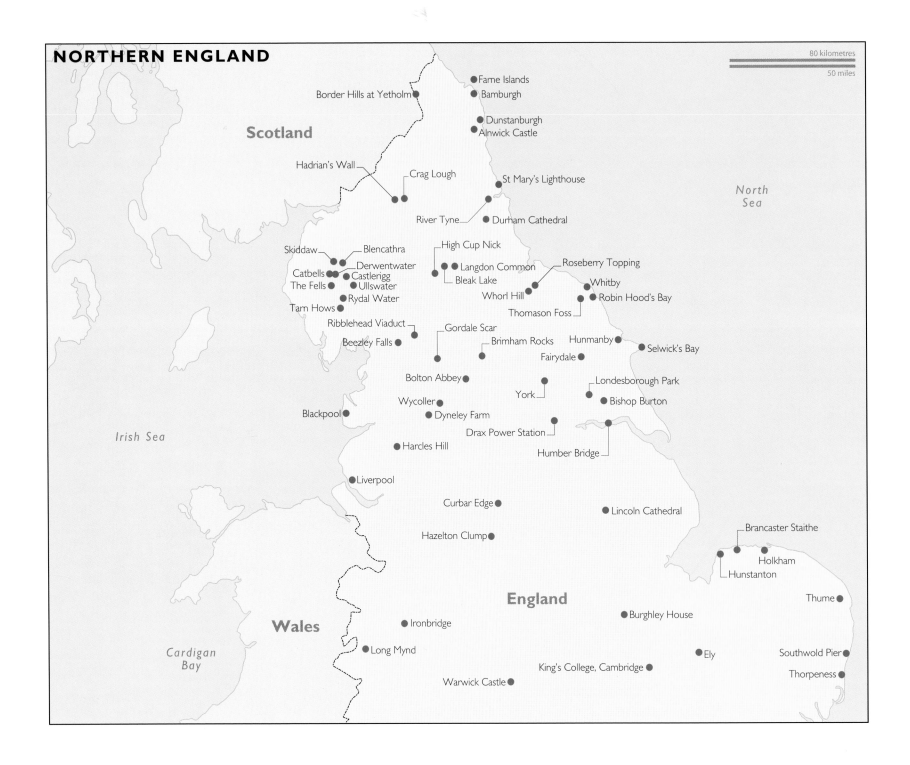

NORTHERN ENGLAND

80 kilometres

50 miles

Scotland

England

Wales

North Sea

Irish Sea

Cardigan Bay

Fame Islands
Border Hills at Yetholm
Bamburgh
Dunstanburgh
Alnwick Castle
Hadrian's Wall
Crag Lough
St Mary's Lighthouse
River Tyne
Durham Cathedral
High Cup Nick
Skiddaw
Blencathra
Derwentwater
Langdon Common
Roseberry Topping
Catbells
Castlerigg
Bleak Lake
Whitby
The Fells
Ullswater
Whorl Hill
Robin Hood's Bay
Rydal Water
Thomason Foss
Tarn Hows
Ribblehead Viaduct
Gordale Scar
Hunmanby
Beezley Falls
Brimham Rocks
Selwick's Bay
Fairydale
Bolton Abbey
Londesborough Park
York
Wycoller
Bishop Burton
Blackpool
Dyneley Farm
Drax Power Station
Harcles Hill
Humber Bridge
Liverpool
Curbar Edge
Lincoln Cathedral
Hazelton Clump
Brancaster Staithe
Holkham
Hunstanton
Thume
Burghley House
Ironbridge
Long Mynd
Ely
Southwold Pier
King's College, Cambridge
Thorpeness
Warwick Castle

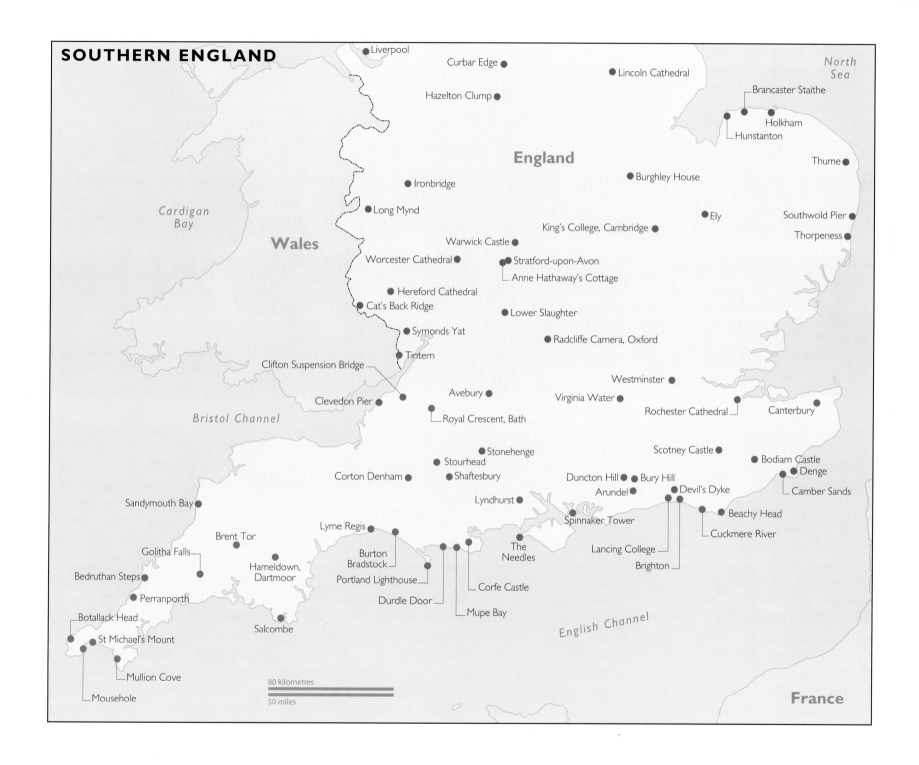

SOUTHERN ENGLAND

England

Wales

France

Cardigan Bay

Bristol Channel

English Channel

North Sea

Liverpool
Curbar Edge
Lincoln Cathedral
Hazelton Clump
Brancaster Staithe
Holkham
Hunstanton
Thume
Ironbridge
Burghley House
Long Mynd
Ely
Southwold Pier
King's College, Cambridge
Thorpeness
Warwick Castle
Worcester Cathedral
Stratford-upon-Avon
Anne Hathaway's Cottage
Hereford Cathedral
Cat's Back Ridge
Lower Slaughter
Symonds Yat
Radcliffe Camera, Oxford
Tintern
Clifton Suspension Bridge
Westminster
Avebury
Virginia Water
Clevedon Pier
Rochester Cathedral
Canterbury
Royal Crescent, Bath
Stonehenge
Scotney Castle
Stourhead
Bodiam Castle
Corton Denham
Shaftesbury
Denge
Duncton Hill
Bury Hill
Arundel
Camber Sands
Sandymouth Bay
Devil's Dyke
Lyndhurst
Beachy Head
Spinnaker Tower
Brent Tor
Cuckmere River
Lyme Regis
Lancing College
Golitha Falls
The Needles
Bedruthan Steps
Burton Bradstock
Brighton
Hameldown, Dartmoor
Portland Lighthouse
Perranporth
Corfe Castle
Botallack Head
Durdle Door
St Michael's Mount
Mupe Bay
Mullion Cove
Salcombe
Mousehole

80 kilometres
50 miles

NOTES ON THE PHOTOGRAPHS

pages 10–11

The secret path, Golitha Woods

I always reckon that half of my images are shot in the place I intended and the other half are shot on the way there. This was firmly in the latter category. The actual Golitha Falls, hidden in a quiet dell on Bodmin Moor, proved too awkward a composition to satisfy my criteria, but this magical burst of sunlight through the heavy summer canopy proved irresistible.

pages 12–13

Classic view of Stourhead

I'm hardly the first person to shoot the classic view down the lake at Stourhead Gardens, so choosing the optimum time of year and timing my exposure to the second was going to be crucial. The October sunlight was flickering in a frustrating manner, but given a few attempts these can often be the most rewarding conditions.

pages 14–15

To sea at Perranporth

Near the end of a couple of weeks moseying around on the two peninsulas at the foot of England, a visit to Perranporth seemed like an afterthought, particularly as the skies were largely drab and unpromising. At the coast though, the unexpected can occur. I watched surfers using the last of the daylight, while I used lines in the wet sand and the rich colour to create a worthwhile seascape.

pages 16–17

Dark Clouds, Clifton Suspension Bridge

Even on the weekend of a friend's wedding in Bristol I somehow managed to sneak away for a few hours with a large camera. The middle of the day was all I could spare, but a few breaks in the heavy cloud presented the opportunity I needed: from the west bank of the River Avon, beneath Brunel's magnificent bridge, the dramatic cliffs on the opposite bank caught in equally dramatic light.

pages 18–19

Footprints at Bedruthan Steps

I first visited Bedruthan at the time of the total eclipse in 1999 with a 35 mm camera and a bag full of hope. The best I achieved was a tiny disc of sun, partially eclipsed, through grey cloud, but the experience (particularly the street lights of Newquay flickering on) and the place stayed with me. It remains one of my most favourite locations in England, and I'm sure I haven't yet exhausted its possibilities.

pages 20–1

Late sunlight on Hameldown, Dartmoor

I was no doubt heading elsewhere on Dartmoor when I caught sight of Hameldown: a wide, flat-topped hill which rises to 530 metres. Given the elevation of the surrounding land, however, its height hardly registers as being of interest to a photographer. With dramatic bursts of summer-evening light and thunderous clouds beyond, though, any location can reveal a certain glory.

pages 22–3

Summer cloud above Brent Tor

Dartmoor offers a wealth of photographic opportunities and I'm indebted to fellow panoramic photographer and friend, David Entrican, for alerting me to particular locations. Given his many excellent photographs of it, I suspect David's favourite spot is Brent Tor. Thwarted on top of the outcrop, I had some luck looking lazily upwards from near the car park.

pages 24–5

Sublime dawn, Salcombe

The view of Salcombe from Snapes Point is sublime. Once again, though, I relied on the work of another photographer, Richard Downer, to point me in the right direction. On my first morning there, Richard and David Entrican, who were on the beach at East Portlemouth across the estuary, exchanged texts with me on how poor the conditions were. The very next dawn, though, I struck gold.

pages 26–7

Sunrise beyond Corfe Castle

The ruins of Corfe Castle seem to have been designed to appeal to painters, poets and photographers. A May morning required a very early start, but I was in position to see the sun rise above the mist. When it became too bright, I jogged around to the eastern side of the castle mound where I found at least five other photographers. I feel I made the right choice with my first location.

pages 28–9

Rock lines at Mupe Bay

Mupe is a hidden gem of the astonishing Dorset coastline. Surrounded by military firing ranges, it is only accessible to the public at certain times. Even in rather murky conditions it proved delightful. My simply composition makes use of the natural lines in the rock and the faint light catching the cliffs at Worbarrow to the east. I hope the bombs always fall elsewhere!

pages 30–1

Royal Crescent in autumn, Bath

Built in the late-eighteenth century, Royal Crescent makes me wonder why more of England's residential architecture could not have aspired to such high ideals. Although I use a wide angle camera, the whole crescent presents a vista too wide even for me. I settled for a pleasing combination of skies and shadow, as the sun hit the terrace one November afternoon.

pages 32–3

Sculpted cliffs, Burton Bradstock

Nothing in England lasts forever, and here at Burton Bradstock in Dorset, the beach of coarse sand is gradually being washed away and these magnificent cliffs are coming under increased attack from the waves. Already the sandstone is being undercut, creating wonderful natural sculptures. The figure of a lone fisherman retiring for the day offers a useful sense of scale.

pages 34–5
Evening light, Avebury stone circle
Stonehenge is England's most celebrated stone circle, but at Avebury you can really get in amongst it. The outer ring is well over 300 metres wide and surrounds part of the village. The Barber Stone, closest to the camera, is alleged to have collapsed onto a man digging beneath it in the fourteenth century. For 600 years, his bones have lain beneath the stone. I didn't like to get too close, even if the story is disputed!

pages 36–7
Gold Hill, Shaftesbury
I loved Gold Hill long before I picked up a camera, thanks to the talented Sir Ridley Scott, who filmed his celebrated Hovis advertisement there in 1973. Sir Ridley achieved better light than I did, though I suspect he allowed himself more time! On another occasion I shot the same scene in heavy snow, but I prefer the unexpectedly warm colour of the cottages on this dull April day.

pages 38–9
Intense spray at The Cobb, Lyme Regis
The Cobb at Lyme Regis is mercifully – and quite surprisingly – still free of the trappings of today's health and safety culture. Although I was spared the crashing waves braved by Meryl Streep in *The French Lieutenant's Woman*, the fine spray and a strong wind forced me to wipe the filters on the camera immediately before every shot. Even so, all that water produced an unmistakably soft-focus effect.

pages 40–1
St Andrew's, Corton Denham
The glorious village of Corton Denham in Somerset lies tucked in to the south of a high wold. Fellow panoramic photographer David Noton has taken a wonderful wide-angle shot of the village dusted in snow. While artists and photographers have always borrowed from one other, straightforward copying is frowned on. Happily I managed to find my own pleasing telephoto composition of the parish church.

pages 42–3
The Scovarn Rock, Mullion Cove
Shooting in Cornwall was unexpectedly stressful. Typically English summer weather – warm, but with plenty of haze and high cloud – made sharp and pleasing light a very rare commodity. Mullion Cove was one of the few places where I felt relaxed; a simple shot of the harbour and a benign sea in the early evening from the cliff above the Scovarn Rock provided this surprisingly good result.

pages 44–5
Boats at Mousehole Harbour
Foreground detail is rarely the forte of panoramic cameras, but at Mousehole this unintended sculpture of small boats propped up against the harbour wall offered an ideal array of surfaces for the eye to pan across. As the summer sun rose hazily, my unending search for dazzling light in Cornwall appeared likely to be frustrated once again, but the day had at least begun well.

pages 46–7
The tin mines of Botallack Head
Sites where old industrial structures, like these tin mines at Botallack Head, are beginning to merge back into the landscape are often of interest to me. In this case, I was amazed to discover an old greetings card which showed exactly the view I'd been hoping for. Although the grey clouds shifted, the sun flatly refused to emerge, but the patterned sky and the swell on the rocks offered enough to produce a result.

pages 48–9
Clevedon Pier at sundown
Clevedon has one of the largest ranges from high to low tide in the world. On my first visit with the big camera, the tide was in, preventing any worthwhile perspective on the elegant Victorian pier. I returned as an afterthought, on the way back to Cornwall in early 2010. This time the tide was out and the skies clear so I took up position in the thick tidal mud waiting for the sun to decline.

pages 50–1
Durdle Door and the coast path, Isle of Purbeck
Durdle Door is one of the great icons of the English coastline, if not coastlines the world over. Curiously, before my first visit I was told by someone that the arch had collapsed. However, when I checked with my own eyes a few weeks later, I found it magnificently intact, and looking strong enough to weather a few more winter storms. One day though, sadly, it will be gone.

pages 54–5
Autumn evening, Bolton Abbey
Shooting with two friends, I spotted a potential opportunity and crossed the River Wharfe without them. Although now shooting into the sun, I was able to shoot through the trees to protect to protect the film from flare. As the sun went down it spread delightful, warm light onto the trees below the ridge. The Abbey itself was in shadow, but this was hardly an opportunity to be missed.

pages 56–7
Holy Trinity Church, Stratford-upon-Avon
In early 2005, we were still in the middle of one of the drabbest and greyest winters I could remember, but things brightened up remarkably for a single morning while I happened to be visiting Stratford. The colours, vivid despite the winter, were clearly reflected in the river (blurred here by a longer exposure). Across the river lies the final resting place of William Shakespeare. It was a morning he might have appreciated.

pages 58–9
Ironbridge in autumn
Ironbridge is one of the most impressive of the many monuments to a time when England led the world in engineering and technology. On a previous visit, summer sunlight on the bridge had proved too strong and direct. This autumn day offered only grey, diffuse light, but that can be ideal for capturing autumn colour. Autumnal leaves, hanging from a foreground tree, appeared to be falling in the breeze

pages 60–1
Entrance to Gordale Scar
My intention, on this bright, fresh spring day, was to photograph the inner reaches of Gordale Scar with its towering cliffs and waterfalls. My favourite image, however, was taken within ten minutes of leaving the car on the walk to the entrance to the gorge. The dry stone wall and edges provide a fine composition, while the flickering light beneath fast–moving clouds adds further depth.

pages 62–3
Golden Light on Curbar Edge
Curbar Edge is easily accessible, but some prefer to do it the hard way. I spotted the nylon rope of a group of climbers, but, unfortunately, the climbers themselves did not appear until the sun had descended too far to light them, making my shot rather drab. Ten minutes earlier, however, sunlight spilling into the valley below had made the autumnal trees glow like burnished gold.

pages 64–5
Sunburst over Hazelton Clump
A heavy snowfall was melting fast in the Derbyshire sunshine. I had spent the day walking in Dovedale with fellow photographer Richard Brocklesby. Richard had already left and I wasn't expecting to find another shot, but as the sun declined it fell into a band of broken cloud near the horizon, making a final shot of the trees of Hazelton Clump to the south-west possible.

pages 66–7
Morning cloud, the Long Mynd
I only discovered the Long Mynd on my third visit to Shropshire. Here the land rises 500 metres from the plain, above the village of Church Stretton, nestled among the Shropshire Hills. I had intended to visit a number of locations, but spent most of my time driving up and down the Long Mynd. This was taken from one of the few places where the view stretches all the way north to The Wrekin.

pages 68–9
Ribblehead Viaduct from Batty Moss
I'm often appalled by the impact of man-made structures on the landscape, but here the reverse is true: the Ribblehead Viaduct is one of my favourite places in England. Curiously, although I have shot this scene a number of times since, this was taken on my very first visit, on a chilly, breezy November day. The light was hardly ideal, but the view from Batty Moss gives an excellent sense of scale.

pages 70–1
Autumn dawn at Symonds Yat
There's no doubt that autumn is the time to shoot at Symonds Yat Rock. As well as spectacular colour in the trees, there's always a chance that at dawn the curling River Wye will be shrouded in mist after a clear night, due to the peculiarities of air pressure at this time of year. Here the mist had almost completely evaporated by the time the trees on the west bank were in adequate sunlight.

pages 72–3
Hereford Cathedral and the River Wye
Hereford, too, lies on the River Wye, many miles and countless meandering bends upstream from Symonds Yat. Here, the river is broad and, as a rule, calm, as the single boat reveals. The wonderful cathedral houses the Mappa Mundi, a medieval map of the world as it was understood in the fourteenth century. It could give me a few ideas for other locations if I were ever to exhaust the British Isles.

pages 74–5
The River Wye at Tintern
A final image from the beautiful River Wye, not too far from where it feeds into the Severn Estuary at Chepstow. Here, I'm standing in Wales, near the ruins of Tintern Abbey, but the opposite bank is England – the river forms the boundary between the countries for many miles. This morning in early October was cool, with a hint of frost, but soon warmed with the unbroken sunshine.

pages 76–7
Winter colours, Lower Slaughter
The Cotswolds are as English as England gets, with beautiful rolling hills and chocolate-box thatched cottages. But that doesn't make it easy to find places to shoot, or to achieve great light. Bourton-on-the-Water, for example, is simply too busy and perhaps just a bit too manicured, but up the road in Lower Slaughter, a gap in the buildings allowed in just enough winter light to endow the scene with a little magic.

pages 78–9
Light on Brimham Rocks
This seemed to be about the only day in a six-week period in 2007 when the grey skies broke. Brimham offers a huge variety of scenes and I shot many of them. In the afternoon the light became more dramatic, creating a contrast between the brightness of the stones and the darkness of the sky.

pages 80–1
Sunrise, Dyneley Farm
Dyneley Farm lies in the hills near Burnley, in Lancashire. It is one of thousands of such farms across England where the land is still worked and livestock reared in much the same way as has been done for hundreds of years. On this dawn a thick band of grey cloud hugged the horizon, but the rising sun managed to pierce it with brilliant rays of light.

pages 82–3
Twilight hues, Blackpool
I first visited Blackpool on a hot and bustling Saturday afternoon in summer. A few days later, however, I returned, determined to photograph its iconic tower, and found the place transformed. Golden light illuminated the promenade tramlines, and, after the sun had set, I found myself on the muddy beach capturing the sublime colours in this shot of the tower and the Lakeland fells behind.

pages 84–5
View from Cat's Back Ridge, Herefordshire
A view from the famous Cat's Back Ridge in rural Herefordshire. Wales is visible to the right of the picture where the Black Mountain ridge looms. This landscape of lush greenery and productive farmland is something all too easy to take for granted, living in England. It's sometimes only when I fly back home that I'm struck by how fertile England is.

pages 86–7
Late sunlight on Liverpool
Evening winter light illuminates the famous Merseyside skyline, seen here from the Seacombe Ferry Terminal on the Wirral. While most now opt for the easy route through the Mersey Tunnel beneath my feet, the ferry still chugs across the water many times a day. The Liver Building, however, still stands proud and distinctive alongside these would-be usurpers.

pages 88–9
Warwick Castle at dawn
Warwick is one of the most beguiling of English towns, with many timber-framed houses dating back to Tudor times. Its impressive castle, on the River Avon, is quite tricky to shoot, given that most of the river bank opposite is taken up by private gardens. Here, having waited on the Castle Bridge for the sun to rise, I cast a shadow, along with the stone pillars of the bridge, onto the late summer foliage.

pages 90–1
Whirlpools, Beezley Falls
Ingleton, in North Yorkshire, is famed for its Waterfalls Walk where the twin rivers, Doe and Twiss, cut through the limestone rocks, forming small canyons and delightful cascades. My favourite is the perfectly proportioned Beezley Falls, shot here in fading light on an autumn day when the sun seldom broke through the clouds. It took a full two-minute exposure to bring the scene out of the shadows.

pages 94–5
Dawn on the dunes, Bamburgh
There has been a fortification on the basalt outcrop at Bamburgh since at least AD 547. A daunting castle still defies the gales blowing in from the North Sea and the sand blasted against its walls. Northumberland is a 'dawn coast' for photographers; I was out and about before 5 a.m. on this day in May, to take up position in the windswept dune grass.

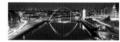

pages 96–7
Blue Millennium, River Tyne
The millennium project to link the town of Gateshead with its neighbouring city of Newcastle to the north enhanced an already impressive urban riverside, possibly England's finest. Although I have photographed the Tyne bridges on numerous occasions, this was an early attempt from the centre of the Tyne Bridge itself, using a tungsten-balanced film manufactured by Fuji.

pages 98–9

Blencathra from Low Rigg

England does not have many large mountains. Only four English peaks would be classified as 'Munros' (a Munro being the Scottish term for a peak of over 3,000 feet) and all of these are in the Lake District. Blencathra lies alongside one of those peaks, Skiddaw, and its unmistakable hump is often my first sight of the Lake District from the A66, so it has a special place in my affections.

pages 100–1

Dawn blues, Place Fell and Ullswater

I often wonder what the best view in England is. Perhaps I have yet to find it – I'd like to believe that actually. But of the views from high points, looking down Ullswater from Gowbarrow must be hard to beat. The fells come together particularly seductively from this point. In this shot, taken before dawn in summer, low cloud rises slowly from the lake creating another feature to entice the eye inwards.

pages 102–3

Border Hills at Yetholm

At Shotton, in Northumberland, one finds oneself in the curious position of being able to look southwards from England into Scotland, towards the Scottish hills and the settlements of Yetholm. On the left is Coldsmouth Hill, steadfastly English – the border is marked by the stone wall stretching to the left. There is little evidence in this peaceful scene of the longstanding, violent rivalry between the two countries.

pages 104–5

The Fells in winter, from Dale Head

Dale Head is not the Lake District's most taxing climb – if you can find somewhere to hide the car at the top of the Honister Pass as I did. It's still a 350-metre slog, but the rewards far outweigh any hardship. I usually walk up here for the view down the Newlands valley to the north, but on this day in early March the clouds were forming complex patterns to the south-west over Pillar and the humps of Scafell beyond.

pages 106–7

Tranquillity, Crag Lough

Crag Lough seems to define tranquillity – although things might be very different in a strong wind! I was there at dawn, hoping for light, but even without it the place was charming. The pinkish highlight on the ridge far beyond made very little difference to my exposures. A light shower of rain created perfect circles in the still water and a faint hissing in the air; I would have liked to have filmed and recorded it.

pages 108–9

Alnwick Castle at dawn

England as whole may lack castles compared with neighbours Scotland and Wales, but Northumberland certainly has its fair share. In addition to the solid coastal fortress of Bamburgh it has the sublime palace of Alnwick Castle, where many scenes in the Harry Potter films have been shot. This shot, taken in June, required an exceptionally early start to the day, though I was able to crawl back into bed before breakfast.

pages 110–11

Clearing rain over Rydal Water

The Fairfield Horseshoe is one of the classic Lakeland walks. When I walked it in the summer of 2009 with three old friends from Sunderland, I'd only really anticipated getting tired, and wet. There were certainly heavy showers, but there was also plenty of dramatic light, particularly in the afternoon as we descended Heron Pike and I was able to shoot Rydal Water and Grasmere.

pages 112–13

First light on Catbells and the Newlands Valley

In late March, there was still a dusting of snow on the fells. Despite my luxury accommodation as a result of a lecture I'd given in Keswick, it was no hardship to leave before dawn as I'd seen the weather forecast. A quick sprint up Skelgill Bank put me in position to capture the rising sun catching the peaks surrounding the Newlands Valley.

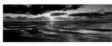

pages 114–15

Sunrise over the Farne Islands

The spectacular Farne Islands are a bumpy boat trip from Seahouses on the Northumbrian coast. I wasn't able to stay on the islands, so was unable to shoot at dawn or dusk, but I did manage to photograph a few of the seabird colonies. This image was taken from the sands between Budle Bay and Bamburgh as the sun rose over the isles, and purple hues in the sky blended with the saturated sands.

pages 116–17

Into the light, Dunstanburgh

Dunstanburgh is the third of Northumberland's great castles. Shooting from the renowned 'cannonball beach' can be tricky; the boulders are large and so can the waves be – even wellies are sometimes inadequate. This dawn in early May provided just enough interest in the sky, but the sunrise was still too far to the south to enliven the castle with light.

pages 118–19

Classic view of Durham Cathedral

Durham Cathedral is quite possibly the finest building in Britain, due in no small measure to its precipitous position on the banks of the River Wear. I took some of my earliest 'landscape' photographs from this point with an instamatic camera, aged around ten. When I first took delivery of a panoramic camera, my first port of call when visiting the North East was the exact same spot. Some views never change.

pages 120–1

Roseberry Topping at dusk

The curiously sculpted Roseberry Topping lies on the northern fringes of the North Yorkshire Moors. It is possible to guess its original shape when one knows that the sharp, westward-facing rock face was created by a collapse in 1914, possibly caused by old mine workings. This was shot from the eastern side of the summit, catching the last burst of sunlight on one of the longest days of the year.

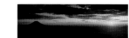

pages 122–3

May morning, Tarn Hows

There's something curiously different about the famous view at Tarn Hows. Somehow it doesn't look like England at all; the tall pines suggest the Alps, or the Canadian Rockies, but there are no soaring mountains beyond, only the more ancient peaks of Langdale and the Helvellyn group. On this bright morning in May, you could almost taste the springtime optimism of this exquisite landscape.

pages 124–5

Snows on Skiddaw, from Skelgill Bank

I'm rarely entirely satisfied with weather conditions; I complain when skies are clear and when there is total cloud cover. In the Lake District, broken cloud is all too common, but this is often when the magic begins, with rapidly changing light. Here a scudding snow cloud coats the summit of Skiddaw, while light passes over Swinside hill in the foreground.

pages 126–7

St Mary's Lighthouse, Whitley Bay

The copywriter who came up with the great line 'Florida's horrider than Whitley Bay' for a television advertisement in my childhood must have ventured up the coast as far as St Mary's Lighthouse. I've always been a fan of lighthouses. Souter, another ten miles to the south was my childhood haunt, but St Mary's, with its tidal causeway is perhaps the most aesthetically pleasing in Britain.

pages 128–9

Summer storms above Hadrian's Wall

On a warm afternoon in early summer, cumulonimbus clouds pile up beyond Peel Crags, threatening thunder and heavy rain. Despite having been built in just six years, Hadrian's Wall, the northernmost outpost of the Roman Empire, has withstood similar weather and much worse, for almost two millennia. It remains perhaps Britain's most remarkable large-scale construction project.

pages 130–1

Lightburst over Lady's Rake, Derwentwater

More than once I've attempted to traverse the crags overlooking Derwentwater and its shoreline in a single day. So far I haven't succeeded – too easily distracted by the views perhaps. In this shot transient light flashes across Catbells on the far side, and shots from the Walla Crag and Lady's Rake were possible, taking in the head of the lake, and even the view behind, towards Blencathra.

pages 132–3

Solitary Tree, High Cup Nick

The Lake District National Park comprises only about a third of Cumbria, England's third largest county. High Cup Nick deserves its own national park, though that might disturb the peace! Ground out by successive ice ages, this perfectly U-shaped valley is tucked into the edge of the Pennine Fells. Despite its awesome scale, it is hidden from view until rounding the corner on the path near Dufton.

pages 134–5

The Bleak Lake, Cow Green Reservoir

Large tracts of England, particularly along the central spine of the Pennines could be described as 'bleak', where moorland cannot be put to any agricultural use, and is all the better for it, but successfully capturing this 'bleakness' can be difficult. Cow Green Reservoir presented an opportunity when, for a minute, shortly before sunset, the sun shone brightly through the grey clouds, almost burning a hole in the film.

pages 138–9

Sharp dawn light, Selwick's Bay

I lived for a few years near the Yorkshire coast and the chalk cliffs of Flamborough and Bempton were a constant attraction. There are a number of superb locations from which to view them. Selwick's Bay is furthest east, beneath the lighthouse. Here, the September sun was clipping the nearer cliff as it rose, casting a shadow, but still lighting the northern cliff of the bay with brilliant yellow light.

pages 140–1

Autumn on the city walls, York

Eboracum, Jorvik and now York: the walled city reveals in the history of its name how cultures and civilizations have succeeded one another in England for thousands of years. Today's commuters scurry home through walls built by the Romans. In the background, magnificent York Minster built on the site of the original Roman fortress, catches some golden light.

pages 142–3

Sunrise, Whorl Hill from Scarth Wood Moor

The North York Moors meet the Vale of York here at Red Scarth Moor, near the village of Swainby. Interrupting the view is the small, but beautifully rounded Whorl Hill. Dawn provided very little in the way of direct sunlight and the moors blocked much of the early light, but the clouds seemed to blend with the land in a sublime composition. Perhaps it is hard to take a bad photograph here.

pages 144–5

Light on the mud, Humber Estuary

The Humber Bridge, completed in 1981, has been regarded as a failure in commercial terms. To my mind, from an aesthetic point of view it is a tremendous success. Up close, the concrete can overwhelm, but from a distance, the bridge appears slender and elegant. Here the mudflats near Barton-upon-Humber reflect the sky, while rotting wooden posts offer a reminder of how the river was once crossed.

pages 146–7

Evening light, Drax, from Long Drax

My photographic interests are not restricted to the natural landscapes of England, nor only to its finest architecture. There is something about the scale of England's coal-fired power stations which has always impressed me. Drax is the largest, producing about 7 per cent of the UK's electricity – and an equivalent percentage of its carbon emissions.

pages 148–9

September skies, Burghley House

I'm not generally a great admirer of stately homes. Architecturally speaking, most of them are actually rather conformist and some quite brash, even ugly. A few do stand out, though: Castle Howard being one and Burghley House another, both of which reveal individuality and delicacy in their design. Burghley seems a perfect blend of power and poise, complemented here by autumnal blue skies.

pages 150–1

Frosted dawn, Londesborough Park

This is the image closest to my home in East Yorkshire. Londesborough Park features a small lake, a rarity on these chalk wolds. Perhaps it was this lake which caused the rising sun to be shaded by mist but the haze appears to continue further into the scene, which is unusual for such a cold morning. It's also rare with a panoramic camera to find quite such an ideal foreground as the frosted plants which frame the image.

pages 152–3

Sunrise at Southwold Pier

Famous, in recent years, as Gordon Brown's holiday destination of choice, Southwold is popular for being one of the driest and sunniest places in England and the sunshine appears to have made the town a cheery place. Here the sun rises in spring above the groynes which buttress the town against the waves; many settlements further north have long since been abandoned to the sea.

pages 154–5

Hot and cold, Fairydale

An aerial view of the Yorkshire Wolds reveals strange curving 'scars' on the landscape. These are chalk valleys, carved out by streams that have long since disappeared, while the flattened ridge tops have been cultivated by farmers. My favourite chalk valley is probably Fairydale, near the tiny village of Fimber, where the valley curves away into the distance, overlooked by a uniform line of trees.

pages 156–7

Light at Brancaster Staithe

Having been raised on the north-east coast of England, I found the northern coast of Norfolk strange. Both Wells and Cley claim to be 'next-the-Sea', but the sea is nowhere to be seen! Saltmarsh, sand, mud and reed beds would be more than welcome at Happisburgh, where lines of houses are gradually falling into the sea. Here, at Brancaster Staithe, there is space to leave your boat and forget about it.

pages 158–9

Summer cloud, King's College, Cambridge

A white cow grazes on the Backs as summer cloud piles up beyond King's College Chapel. Earlier, I had watched students celebrating their graduation with drinks on the lawn. The day was about as hot and dusty as England gets and I could have used one of those drinks myself, but had to make do later with a bottle of water while I sat on King's Parade as rain began to douse the streets.

pages 160-1

Autumn glory, Bishop Burton

There are many wonderful villages that I could have photographed, but after largely unsuccessful attempts at more famous locations such as Castle Coombe, Dunster and Lacock, I found that Bishop Burton, within ten miles of my home, would best represent this enduring aspect of England. A broad horse chestnut tree embraces the whitewashed houses, while late sunshine highlights golden leaves on the village green.

pages 162-3

Sky drama, Lincoln Cathedral

Although born in Lincoln, I had left at the age of three. It was great to be afforded the opportunity to shoot the cathedral from the castle walls. I had tried a number of angles before and hadn't been satisfied with the results. My father was with me and I could sense his boredom as I waited for the optimum moments to release the shutter on a superb afternoon of broken cloud. I'm pleased I made him wait.

pages 164-5

Shimmering tides, Hunstanton

Despite being on the east coast, the two-tone cliffs at Hunstanton face west, and so catch the evening sun. For this shot the tide needed to be far enough out to access the beach comfortably around sunset. As the tide sneaked in, shimmering between the stones, I skipped from boulder to boulder waiting for the best moments to click the shutter. I still had plenty of time to find my way back to the promenade, though.

pages 166-7

Summer light in Ely

Unusually, I arrived in Ely for the first time by train, from London. While eating an ice cream, I contemplated shooting the West Tower, but decided that the shot was a little too awkward for my lens. I found what I wanted in a simple shot taken from the park to the south, carefully positioning the trees and making use of patches of white daisies. The result was an unmistakably English scene.

pages 168-9

Late summer skies at Whitby Harbour

Curiously, Bram Stoker used to visit Whitby for his summer holidays rather than during the depths of winter, though he may nevertheless have experienced some tempestuous weather, even in August. This shot was taken from the western side of the harbour, as the sun sank in September. This view of St Mary's church won't have changed greatly since Stoker's day, give or take a few houses and the breakwater.

pages 170-1

Twin storms, Hunmanby, East Yorkshire

This image was taken in the wolds of Hunmanby in late August, just down the road from where we were living at the time. I spotted at least three large clouds promising a deluge and lightning, yet where I stood remained perfectly dry and sunny and the thunderheads gradually dispersed over the North Sea to the east. As someone who often stands in open fields with a large metal tripod I'm always wary of lightning!

pages 172-3

Winter majesty, Robin Hood's Bay

Regarded by many as the jewel of the Yorkshire Coast, the whole bay, stretching all the way to Ravenscar, has long fascinated me. I've taken many different shots of the bay, but this is the classic tourist brochure view. Snow rarely clings to the coast for very long thanks to the constant temperature of the sea, which barely changes between summer and winter, particularly if the sun emerges – as here.

pages 176-7

Cloud forms beyond Beachy Head

The tallest chalk cliff in England welcomes voyagers from across the English Channel. The lighthouse below was opened in 1902 to protect ships after the nearby Belle Tout light on the clifftop was deemed inadequate. Here I shot looking east, as clouds finally broke after a frustrating spell of thumb-twiddling. This is the most familiar English landscape to many of those visiting these shores for the first time.

pages 178-9

Autumn colours at Scotney Castle

Autumn provides a wealth of colour for landscape photographers, and Scotney offers a veritable rainbow, even when shooting early in October. The cylindrical tower is part of the 'old castle', originally one of four. Today the site is a charming amalgam of castle, manor house and exquisitely managed gardens. This view across the moat is perhaps the finest, but there are many other possibilities.

pages 180-1

Mary and Joseph, Camber Sands

On the long expanse of sand at Camber I found a horse called Mary, and a rider called Joseph. No joke. During film shoots, the beach has doubled for Normandy during the D-Day landings, and even the Sahara Desert, so I guess most things are possible here. Joseph was kind enough to spend a few minutes posing for me as a violet afterglow signalled the end of the day. Action shots are not my speciality!

pages 182-3

The Cascade, Virginia Water

Virginia Water and this cascade are entirely man-made, the lake having been created in 1753. It is sufficiently old to appear almost entirely natural, given the water that has flowed over the stones at the top of the falls for so many years. If one ignores the uniform stones at the base, the waterfall resembles many I have shot in the Yorkshire Dales or on the North York Moors.

pages 184-5

Sound mirrors of Denge, Dungeness

The huge shingle beach of Dungeness continues for a few miles up the coast to Denge, where flooded gravel pits help to protect the bizarre modernist sculpture of the sound mirrors. Built in the 1920s, these once had a practical use – they were intended to detect incoming enemy aircraft. In practice they barely worked, but the knowledge gained did help with the techniques used in radar detection.

pages 186-7

Mist on the River Arun, Arundel

Arundel Castle is an imposing hillside fortress, but from this point on the River Arun, on a misty morning in early summer, the view is considerably softened. Only the uppermost tower of the castle is visible, but the view to the small but exquisite cathedral is unhindered. Just off the busy A27, Arundel remains a peaceful oasis, and a beautifully evocative corner of England.

pages 188-9

Morning sunlight, Lancing College

The chapel at Lancing College evokes comparisons with Arundel Cathedral, given that they were both built in the 1860s during the Gothic revival. The building, visible for miles from the nearby main road, eventually drew me in. Thick morning mist was hanging over the nearby River Adur, and a thin veil hung over the college. Later, as the mist finally cleared, I shot the old bridge at Shoreham.

pages 190-1

Radcliffe Camera and St Mary's Church, Oxford

Cities are always tricky to shoot with a panoramic camera, unless there are obvious vantage points. You can look across the dreaming spires of Oxford from the surrounding hills, but I found the view a little distant for my lenses. Instead I elected to get into the heart of the city and shoot the famous Radcliffe Camera of the Bodleian Library, here looking up at the church of St Mary.

pages 192–3

Cloud motif from Devil's Dyke, South Downs

The South Downs, of which Devil's Dyke is part, have recently been confirmed as England's tenth national park. The Dyke is a chalk valley, similar to Fairydale in the Yorkshire Wolds. Here, the view is northwards from the top of the Dyke, across the vast plain of pasture land that stretches 40 miles to the North Downs. It was a beautiful morning, with a fog gradually burning off in the sunshine.

pages 194–5

Durham clinch the title, Canterbury

The St Lawrence ground had always looked wonderful to me in evening sunlight, its famous lime tree casting shadows within the boundary rope. Sadly, the tree has been replaced by a small sapling, but the ground retains plenty of character. The image shows Callum Thorp steaming in to bowl. He collected seven wickets on the third afternoon, helping my beloved Durham to their first ever County Championship title.

pages 196–7

Wild ponies of the New Forest, Lyndhurst

I'm far from being a wildlife photographer – this image is probably the closest I'll ever get! It's difficult to visit the New Forest, though, without trying to photograph the famous resident ponies. On a previous visit to Lyndhurst, I'd managed only a rather gloomy image of Bolton's Bench. Today, however, the sun put in a brief appearance, while dark cloud shifted beyond and the ponies grazed, unconcerned.

pages 198–9

Dawn frost at Bodiam Castle

Ask a child to draw a castle, and he or she will probably draw Bodiam. Its form is perfect: towers, gatehouse, moat, battlements. It never did see much in the way of warfare, which partially accounts for its state of preservation, externally at least. It's a magical place, where it's hard not to imagine one has been transported back to the middle ages. This frosty morning in late February provided ideal conditions.

pages 200–1

Morning skies, Rochester Cathedral

Unlike Bodiam, Rochester Castle, from where this photograph was taken, has seen much action; including two sieges in the thirteenth century, when the cathedral was twice looted. Things are relatively peaceful these days, apart from the bustling city. On this fine morning, while parties of schoolchildren arrived to absorb the local history, I made use of the fine skies and wisps of white cloud.

pages 202–3

Dawn shadows at Stonehenge

England's most famous ancient monument stands on an otherwise unremarkable plain, near Amesbury in Wiltshire. Opinions differ as to when the stones were erected, but that so many still stand today is testament to the importance afforded the site throughout many ages. I used the shallow ditches and mounds to the north of the circle to create depth in the image, while the March sun gradually thawed the frost.

pages 204–5

Westminster and the London Eye from Jubilee Bridge

Due to the South Bank's many floodlights, it's a great place to shoot at night. The lights are reflected by and spread on the flowing river. Near the London Eye, on the Jubilee footbridge, is a great spot to look towards the Palace of Westminster. Night-time photography can often be hit and miss, but here it becomes a pleasure.

pages 206–7

The Needles from Alum Bay, Isle of Wight

On my visit to the Isle of Wight the sky was flat and grey with no useful light. It's amazing how often perseverance can pay off in such conditions, even if the local tourist board is unlikely to be interested in the images. Fellow photographer and local, Ian Scovell, helped me to find this view from Alum Bay towards The Needles. Colour on the rocks and in the sea compensates for anything lacking in the sky.

pages 208–9

Spring glory at Duncton Hill

A moment of magic on the South Downs. The view from Duncton Hill is partially obscured by trees, but my lens was ideal for using them to frame the scene on each side. The last beams of sunlight brought brilliant colour to the foliage, and shafts of light picked out the trees below.

pages 210–11

The West Pier at Brighton

Brighton's West Pier had been derelict for a number of years before a succession of calamities hit the structure in 2003, including a major fire. The rusting skeleton quickly became a magnet for photographers. Here, in April, the pier is lit by the final rays of light from the west. In the far distance, the East Pier continues to pull in business, while a tower is planned for the West Pier entrance site on the promenade.

pages 212–13

Storm shadows, Bury Hill

A dead tree stands in this field on upper Bury Hill on the South Downs, above the village of Amberley. I photographed this scene under various different conditions. Small features of the English landscape occasionally grab hold of me and won't let me go until I'm satisfied I've captured them to the best of my ability. The tree won't remain forever, but few things do in England's constantly changing landscape.

To tackle this huge England project, I used pretty much the same equipment as for my previous publications. My workhorses are a couple of old G617 cameras, with a fixed 105 mm lens (my favourite all-round lens) and a Fotoman kit with 90 mm and 180 mm Rodenstock lenses, along with a 300 mm Fuji lens. I also intermittently tested a number of Fuji GX617 cameras and various lenses for them, while buying and selling them as part of my business. I still use Velvia 50 film for most shots, save a small number on RTP 64, Velvia 100f and Provia 400. Processing was, as ever, by the fantastic Bob Harvey at NPS Media in Middlesbrough. To balance the light on the film I use the indispensable Pentax digital spotmeter in conjunction with Lee filters, in particular the neutral density hard and soft grads, warm-up filters and polarizer. The cameras are almost always balanced on top of Manfrotto tripods.

Nothing ever goes entirely smoothly. I arrived for a week to shoot the south-west corner of the country with plans to cover Essex, and some parts of Sussex which I wanted to revisit. As I was walking into the hotel a strap gave way on my 18 kg camera bag and it fell a short distance on to the ground. I foolishly thought little of it at the time – there was no apparent damage to my cameras – and carried on, undaunted. I shot the fishing boats in the mud of Leigh-on-Sea, a view from the hill overlooking the pier at Southend, the frosted grass at Bodiam Castle, and a breaking cloudscape over the Cuckmere River. Sadly, none of these images ever existed other than in my viewfinder. The shutter of the oldest and dearest of my 617 cameras had been broken, and it had remained firmly closed throughout the week. As it was a camera with a viewfinder, rather than a mirror or a ground glass, there was no way to tell that this had happened other than by looking through the shutter directly. The unexposed film remained a decidedly doleful black, rather than the vivid colours of the south of England that I'd anticipated. Four-fifths of the 'images' I had shot that week had been lost. I took the setback rather in my stride, I thought, dismissing it as merely an expensive mistake, whereas earlier in my career I would probably have been distraught. I repeated the week's work and, in some cases, found new and exciting subjects. There are more important things to worry about than a few photographs that never existed – though these days I do check my shutters on a regular basis!

To view the rest of the photographs taken during this five-year England project and
for limited edition prints of images from this book visit: www.markdentonphotographic.co.uk

With thanks to:

Rachel, Lucy, Sam, Kate and Gregan, Rebecca and Szabolcs, Anne, Mike and Myfanwy.

Bob, Ian, Margaret and all at NPS Media, Graham Merritt at Lee Filters, Pete Duncan and Duncan Proudfoot at Constable & Robinson, Richard Downer, David Entrican, Joe Cornish, David Noton,
John Morrison, Pete Leeming, David Marshall, Richard Brocklesby, Ian Scovell.

Colin and Jo Upton, Sharon and Al Lowe, Brian Turnbull, Ian Laws, Stephen Bell, Paul Brown, David Jobling, Anthony Mortimer.